# THE BATMAN STRIKES!

Raintree is an imprint of Capstone Global Library Limited, a company incorporated in England and Wales having its registered office at 7 Pilgrim Street, London, EC4V 6LB - Registered company number: 6695582

First published by Raintree in 2014
The moral rights of the proprietor have been asserted.

Ashley C. Andersen Zantop *Publisher*
Michael Dahl *Editorial Director*
Sean Tulien *Editor*
Heather Kindseth *Creative Director*
Bob Lentz and Hilary Wacholz *Designers*
Tori Abraham *Production Specialist*

DC COMICS
Joan Hilty & Harvey Richards *Original U.S. Editors*
Jeff Matsuda & Dave McCaig *Cover Artists*

ISBN 978 1 406 28567 3

Printed in China.
18 17 16 15 14
10 9 8 7 6 5 4 3 2 1

British Library Cataloguing in Publication Data
A full catalogue record for this book is available from the British Library.

# FROZEN SOLID BY MR. FREEZE!

BILL MATHENY ..................................................WRITER
CHRISTOPHER JONES ...........................PENCILLER
TERRY BEATTY.................................................INKER
HEROIC AGE ...........................................COLOURIST
PAT BROSSEAU ...........................................LETTERER

### BATMAN CREATED BY
### BOB KANE

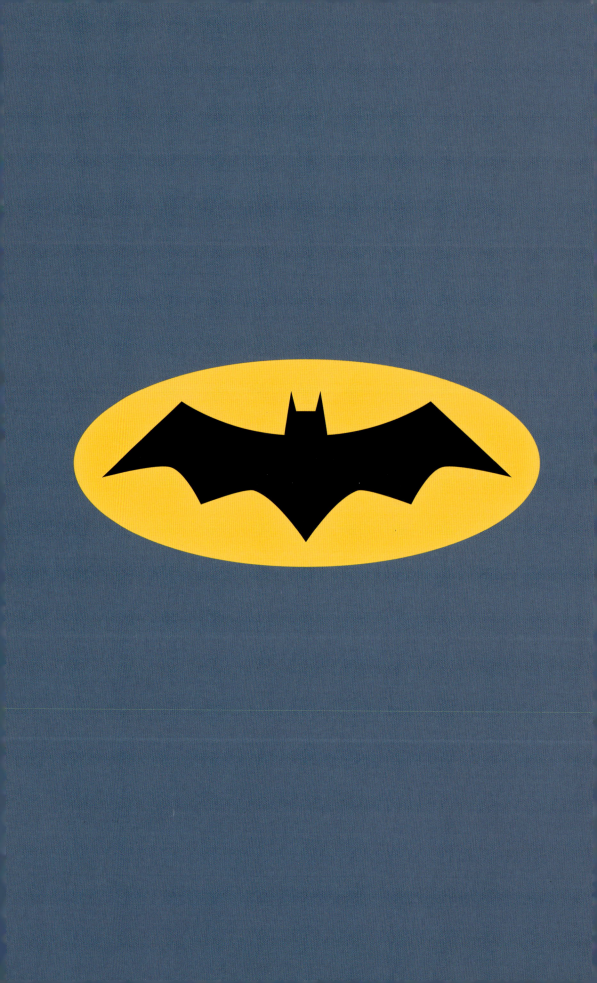

13

BRR. *THANK YOU* FOR THAWING ME OUT.

IT'S NOTHING THAT A FEW MINUTES IN THE *MICROWAVE* COULDN'T CURE.

HMM. *ANTIBIOTICS AND FLUIDS.* I NEVER KNEW YOU HAD SUCH AN IMPRESSIVE *BEDSIDE MANNER.*

I LEARNED FROM THE BEST IN THE BUSINESS.

I WAS *AFRAID* FOR A WHILE THAT I MIGHT LOSE YOU.

YOU NEEDN'T WORRY ABOUT THAT, SIR. I WOULDN'T GIVE THAT *FROSTY FIEND* THE PLEASURE OF MY DEMISE.

I DON'T THINK HE'S HAD A LOT OF TIME TO THINK ABOUT YOU. TAKE A LOOK.

*GOOD HEAVENS!* HE'S CREATED HIS OWN WINTER WONDERLAND BY SEALING OFF THE JEWELRY DISTRICT!

27 LIVE

I HAVE TO *GO* NOW, ALFRED. IT'S TIME TO GET SUITED UP AND END THIS.

AND JUST *HOW* DO YOU PROPOSE TO STOP HIM?

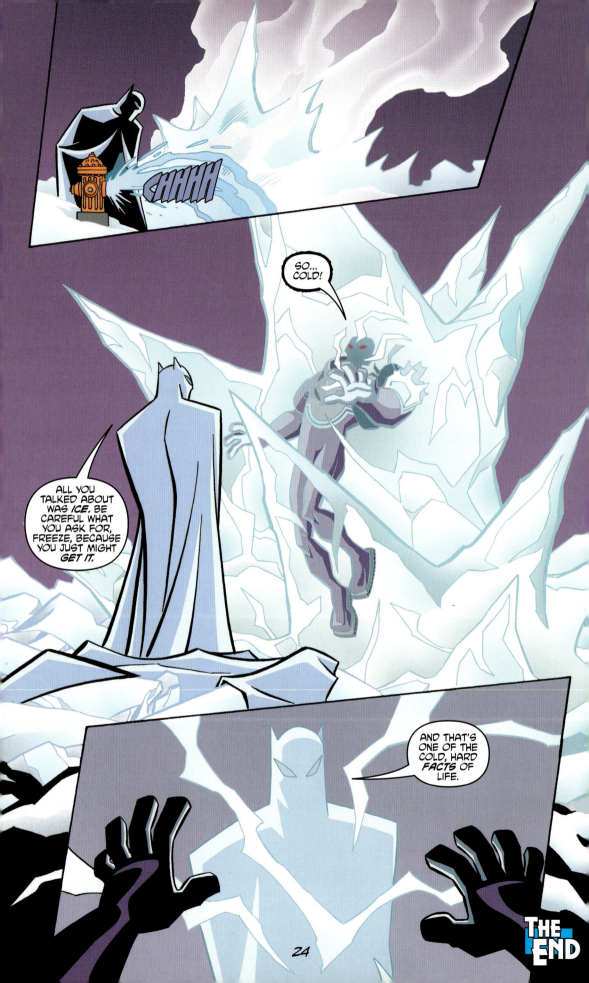

# CREATORS

## BILL MATHENY  WRITER

Along with comics such as THE BATMAN STRIKES, Bill Matheny has written for TV series including KRYPTO THE SUPERDOG, WHERE'S WALDO, A PUP NAMED SCOOBY-DOO, and many others.

## CHRISTOPHER JONES  PENCILLER

Christopher Jones is an artist who has worked for DC Comics, Image, Malibu, Caliber, and Sundragon Comics.

## TERRY BEATTY  INKER

Terry Beatty has inked THE BATMAN STRIKES! and BATMAN: THE BRAVE AND THE BOLD as well as several other DC Comics graphic novels.

# GLOSSARY

**antibiotics** a drug that is used to kill harmful bacteria and to cure infections

**avalanche** a large amount of snow and ice or of dirt and rocks that slides suddenly down the side of a mountain

**demise** death or end

**gravely** seriously or having to do with life and death

**realist** a realist is someone who has accurate or fair expectations

**scheme** a clever and often dishonest plan to do or get something

**seized** took something in a forceful, sudden, or violent way

**solitary** a part of a prison where prisoners are kept alone, or separate from each other

**suave** relaxed, confident, and friendly in social situations

**vicinity** the area around or near a particular place

# VISUAL QUESTIONS & PROMPTS

**1.** Batman's speech bubble has a squiggly tale in this panel. Why does this speech bubble look different than in other panels?

**2.** In this panel we see the Batmobile twice. Why did the comic book's creators do this?

**3.** In the third panel we see the Batmobile overlapping the panel borders. Why did the comic book's creators do this? How does it make you feel?

**4.** In your own words, explain what Batman means when he says that Freeze should be careful what he wishes for.

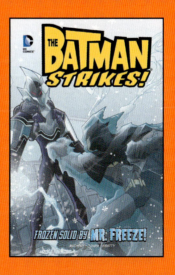